EXTRAORDINARY PROJECTS FROM ORDINARY OBJECTS

JUMBO BOOK VOL #1

A LooLeDo Creation

www.looledo.com
Written and Created by Mark Icanberry

EXTRAORDINARY PROJECTS FROM ORDINARY OBJECTS

JUMBO BOOK VOL #1

Extraordinary Projects from Ordinary Objects Jumbo Book Vol #1
© 2010 by LooLeDo LLC.
All rights reserved
Created by Mark Icanberry
Projects by Mark Icanberry • Written by David Icanberry • Copy Edited by Joan Kresich

I dedicate this book to my son David. Special thanks to my friends and family, and most of all to my wife, for her incredible support, patience, and love.

ISBN 978-1-893327-12-2

Printed in Hong Kong
10 9 8 7 6 5 4 3 2 1

LooLeDo
www.looledo.com

Distributed by LooLeDo, P.O. Box 1202, Alamo, CA 94507

TABLE OF PROJECTS

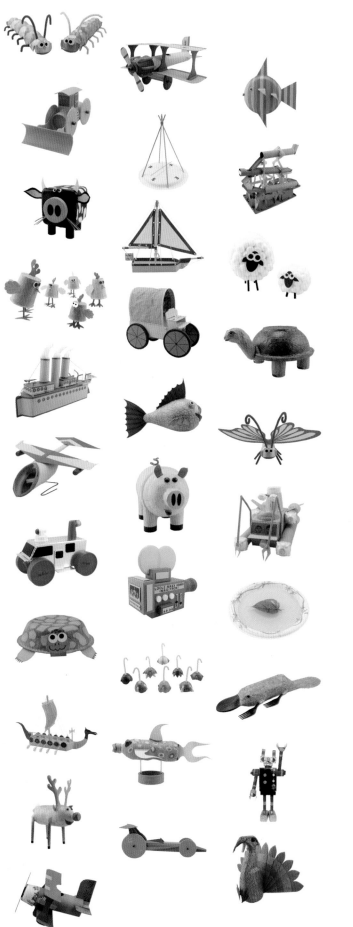

GO GREEN THE LOOLEDO WAY

Saving your supplies

Start recycling the fun way! Save old plastic bottles, milk cartons, paper cups, toilet paper tubes, etc. Keep anything that looks interesting or unusual. I have a big storage bin in my garage that I constantly fill with new materials to build and create with. Its amazing how much we throw away. Re-use everything you can and start saving early.

GETTING STARTED

Getting Started

Pick a project that looks fun to you. This book is designed to help you get creative and use your imagination in new ways. Think outside the box! Or even better...use the box! Get ready to have fun!

Find your materials

It's important to remember that you don't need the exact supplies listed in this book. Use whatever is available to you and get creative if you are missing anything.

Piece it together

I always hold up my pieces and try things out before I tape or glue anything. It's always a good idea to make your changes before you do anything permanent.

Build your project

When building your project, experiment with new and different ways of putting it together. The most important thing is to have fun!

Decorate your creation

You can always decorate your project any way you want. I love masking tape and colored markers but many people enjoy paint, glitter, paper mache, etc. Its the little things that will make your project amazing!

EVERY CRAFT FOR EVERY AGE

Creativity

The goal is creativity! Let the projects be the inspiration, and your children the guide. Young children will naturally make a simplified version, while older ones will have the skills to add details and flouishes.

A simple version

A dressed up version

We are bugging out!

The LooLeBugs are loose in this book and we need your help catching them. How many bugs can you find?

Egg Carton Caterpillars

Find these or similar supplies

- Egg carton
- Masking tape or glue
- Cardboard or construction paper
- Markers or pens for customizing
- Pipe cleaners

Getting Started

1 The first step to building your Egg Carton Caterpillar is cutting out half of an egg carton. Try to trim the sides evenly and be careful not to rip it.

Color it

2 Now its time to color your caterpillar. You can paint it, color it with markers, or glue things onto it. I like to use lots of bright colors for my bugs. Have fun experimenting with the supplies that you have.

Legs

3 Take your pipe cleaners and cut out ten little leg pieces. Tape or glue these pieces inside the egg carton. Try to make the legs the same length, or if you want you can trim them once they are taped into place.

Eyes and antennae

4 Now we need to add the facial features. Cut out two circles of white paper for the eyes and glue them onto the face. Next poke two pieces of pipe cleaner through the back of the head to make the antennae.

Finished

5 VOILÀ! Your Egg Carton Caterpillar is complete, ready to crawl around and eat everything in sight. Have fun!

Big Blazing Biplane

Find these or similar supplies

- 1 paper towel tube
- Cereal box or some cardboard
- Regular masking tape
- Blue tape (to customize it)
- 1 small paper cup
- 6 bendable straws

Getting started

1 Start out by cutting your front wings, tail wing, and tail from a piece of cereal box or cardboard. This is a biplane, so you are going to need two main wings. I played around with their size and shape by drawing them out onto my scrap cardboard before I cut them out. You can get real creative at this point and make your biplane wings look like bird wings or dragon wings!

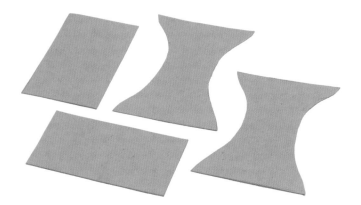

Wing Struts

2 You are going to want to add some kind of support structure between the two front main wings. For the wing struts I simply cut out four rectangles that were all the same size, then trimmed the sides a bit to make them look cool.

Build the engine

3 To make my propeller and motor assembly I punched six holes on the side of a paper cup. I also carefully made a small hole in the center of the bottom of my cup that was slightly bigger than a straw. Trim down your six straws, they will become your exhaust pipes.

Exhaust pipes

4 Now insert your straws into the holes on the sides and trim them as you like. These are the exhaust pipes for your motor. You may need to tape them in place if they don't hold firm on their own.

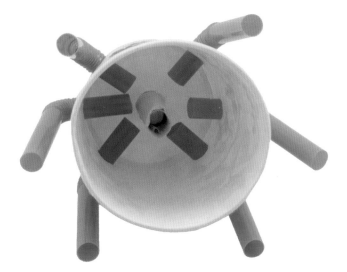

Propeller shaft

5 For my propeller shaft, I took a straight piece of straw and wrapped some tape around one end. Then I inserted it up through the hole on the bottom of my cup.

Propeller

6 My propeller was cut out of an old cereal box. I drew out a design that I liked, cut it out and punched a hole in the center of it. Add some tape to make sure it won't fall off.

Put it together

7 I like to put everything together before I dress it up. This way I can make any changes or alterations before anything is permanent.

Dress it up

8 I covered all of my pieces in tape, using some blue tape to accent certain parts. You could color your plane with markers or paint it if you want.

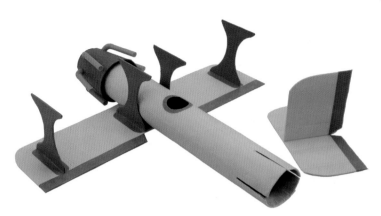

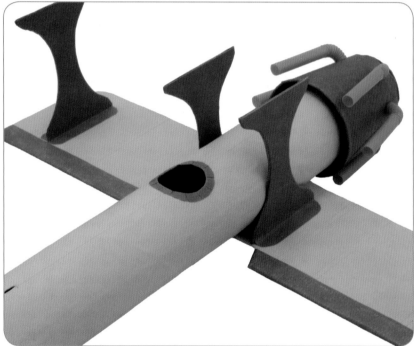

Wing struts

9 Now its time to attach those wing struts to the lower wing. You can also cut a hole in the main body to give your pilot a place to sit. Now you can tape your body to the lower wing.

Attach the tail

10 To attach your tail you will need to cut out three slots first. Cut these out of the back of the paper towel tube. Try to make the cuts as even as possible. Your tail will slide right in.

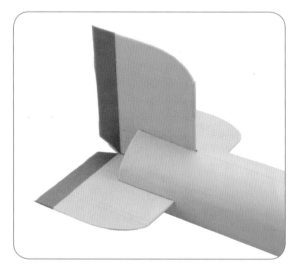

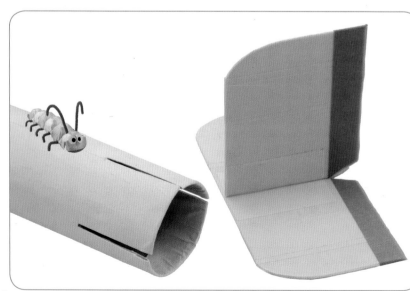

Final touch

11 I added some decals for my wings and some stripes on my propeller. You can add anything you want to your plane, maybe you can draw on some flames or lightning bolts. Have fun and experiment!

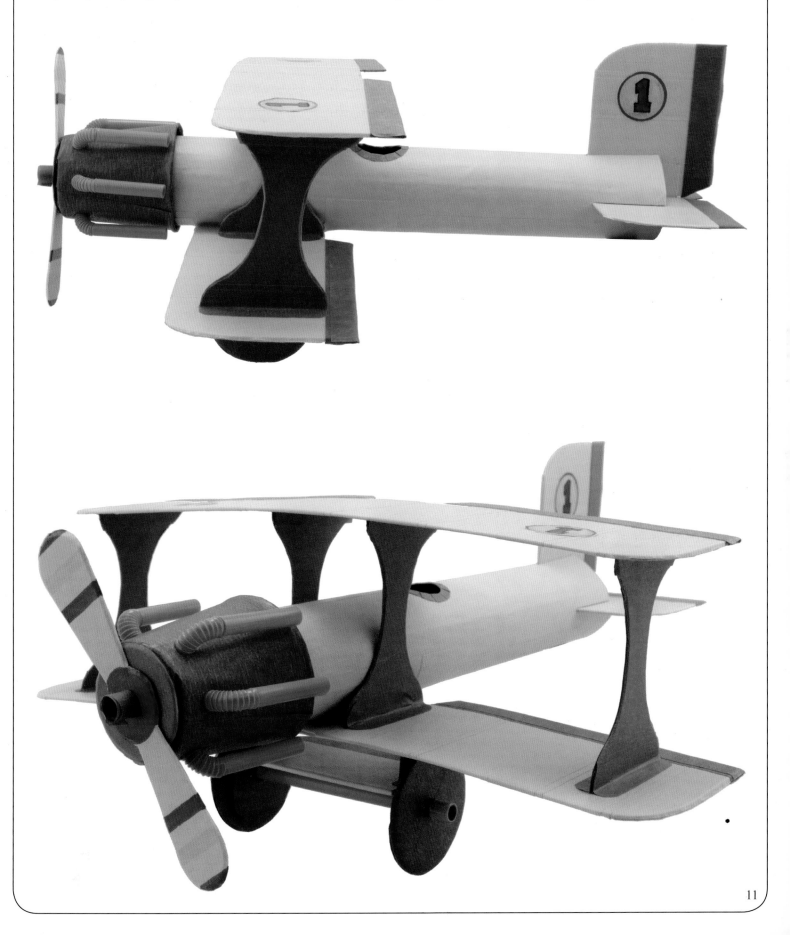

Paper Plate Fish

Find these or similar supplies

- 2 small paper plates
- Old box or cardboard
- Tape for customizing

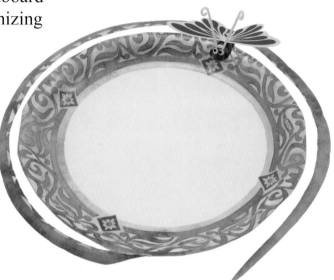

Getting started

1 Start out by trimming both of your paper plates, cutting off the edge that rolls back down. This way when you tape the two halves together, there will be a nice clean edge. I carefully held my paper plates together, facing each other and then cut the excess off.

Fins and tail

2 Next I cut out my fins from an old box. You could play around with different designs, cutting them out and holding them up to your fish body. When you like one, tape it to the inside of one of your paper plates. I added one flipper and two fins.

Attach the plates

3 I attached both paper plates together using my hot glue gun but you could just as easily use tape or regular glue.

Finishing touches

4 At this point you can draw eyes in and use markers to make cool designs on your fish.

Dress it up

5 I used different colors of tape to decorate my fish. You could use markers or paint or anything you'd like on yours. Have fun!

Fish eyes

6 I used some red thumb tacks for my fish's eyes, but you could also use paper circles.

Fish Mouth

7 I stuck a little piece of straw onto the front of my fish to give it a little pucker mouth.

13

The TP Dozer

Find these or similar supplies

- Cereal box or some cardboard
- 2 toilet paper tubes
- 1 or 2 straws
- Tape

Getting started

1 I started out by making my bulldozer blade. Cut one of your toilet paper tubes in half lengthwise.

Make the arms

2 Next you can make the arms that will hold your bulldozer blade. Stand your blade up on to a piece of cardboard and trace out its circular profile. Now decide on a cool arm design and make two matching arms. Make sure to punch a hole in the end of your arms.

Make some holes

3 Now punch four holes in your other toilet paper tube. Try to make the holes as even as possible.

Install the axles

4 The next step is making and installing your wheel axles. Cut out two pieces of straw and slide them into the holes you've punched. The straws need to turn freely, so adjust the size of the holes if needed.

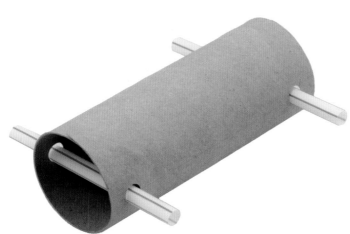

Make the wheels

5 Take an old box or piece of cardboard and draw four circles. Cut these out and punch a hole in the center. Try to make the hole a little smaller than the axle holes.

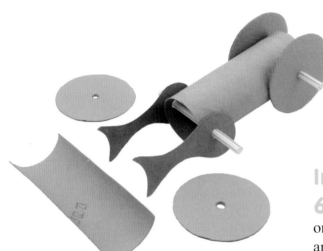

Install the wheels

6 Slide your axle straws through the bulldozer body, then slide on the arms and wheels. Make any adjustments to your wheels, arms, or straws.

Attach the blade

7 All that's left is to attach your front bulldozer blade to both of the arms. Find a position you like and tape the blade on. VOILA! You've built the simple version of the bulldozer!

Tape it up

8 I took all my pieces apart and covered everything with orange masking tape. If you don't have any colored tape you could color your pieces with markers, paint, stickers, or anything you can think of. Use your imagination!

Build a cabin

9 I decided to build a cabin for the driver to sit in! I took a small box and trimmed it to fit on top of my bulldozer. The roof is made from a piece of T.P. tube left over from my bulldozer's blade.

Make some windows

10 To make the windows for my cabin I carefully cut them out of some blue masking tape. You could draw them in place using a colored marker if you like. The door was cut out of cardboard and covered with tape. I added some windows and drew in a little handle and attached it to the cabin.

11 I taped the cabin on, drew in a few steps so that the dozer operator would be able to climb up to the cabin. VOILA! Your T.P. Dozer is complete!

Hanging Compass

Find these or similar supplies

- Magnet (look on the refrigerator)
- Needle or a piece of paper clip
- Thread or thin string
- Small paper plate
- 4 small sticks

Getting started

1 Start out by magnetizing your needle. Any object (like a needle or a paperclip) that sticks to your magnet can be magnetized. With your needle laying down on the table, hold one end down firmly. Then place your magnet onto the needle. Remember, the needle wants to jump to the magnet.

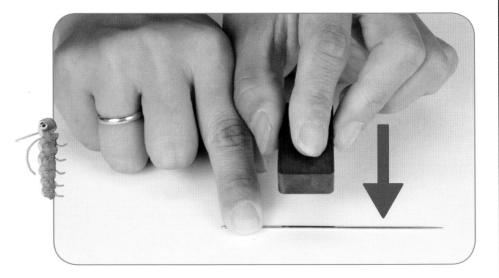

One direction

2 Always slide the magnet in ONE direction along your needle. While holding your needle down, start sliding the magnet away from the finger that you are using to hold it down. Make sure to apply some pressure to the magnet as you slide it along the needle.

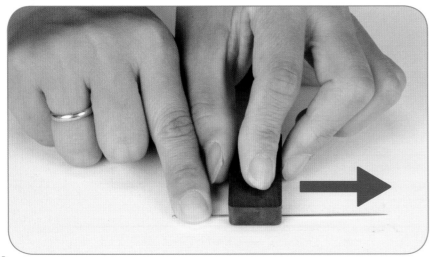

3 KEEP SLIDING

4 ALL THE WAY PAST THE END

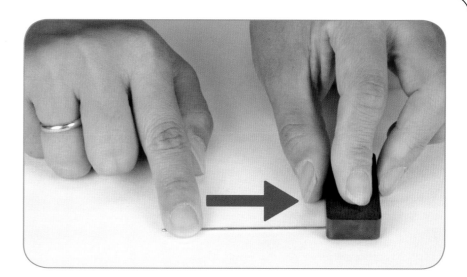

Over again

5 Now lift your magnet up and away from the needle. Bring it around and start all over again. All you are really doing is rubbing the needle in one direction.

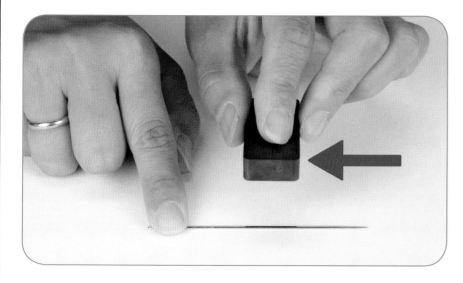

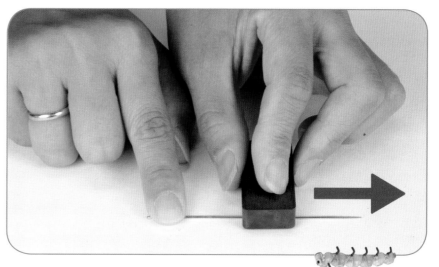

Repeat

6 Repeat step 2 through 5 about 50 times. Yes... that's a lot, but it will insure your needle is properly magnetized. Test to see if your needle is magnetized by touching it to another piece of metal, like another paperclip. If it sticks, then you are ready to make a compass. If not, try magnetizing it again, but rub it more times.

Build the compass

7 OK, now its time to make a compass! I punched four small, evenly-spaced holes on my paper plate, flipped it over, and inserted four small sticks. I then taped them together at the top, now it looks like a tepee!

Next, tie a piece of thread to the needle and attach the other end to the top of the compass stand so that the needle is hanging just above the base. Then very gently slide the thread back and forth on your needle until it is hanging perfectly level. This may take some time, but it is important that the needle is not touching anything. Try to keep everything very still as you do this. Now it should spin and point towards the North.

VOILÀ! A hanging compass! There are all kinds of ways to make compasses, so have fun and try experimenting with different supplies and ways of putting it together!

The Old Mine Shaft Marble Slide

Find these or similar supplies

- Toilet paper tubes
- Paper towel tubes
- Old popsicle sticks or tongue depressors
- Glue gun or tape
- Cardboard or something for your base

Getting started

1 This project is very fun and easy. You can make your marble slide however you'd like, there is no wrong or right way. Just start building and see what you end up with! Start out by cutting most of your toilet paper tubes in half (lengthwise). You can make this project as big or small as you want, so try to judge how many T.P. tubes you'll need beforehand.

Bottom up

2 I decided that the easiest way to build a marble slide is bottom up. Pick the spot you want your marble to come out and start from there. To make your slide you layer your T.P. tubes in an upward angle. I chose the packaging cardboard because it gave me a nice foundation for a big marble slide, but you could use any box or container.

Build it up

3 As your marble slide gets taller you will need to start building a frame. Glue your popsicle sticks to the sides of your box to give your slide more elevation.

Frame

4 I added support as I built my marble slide higher and higher. Its amazing how easy it is to build with glue and some popsicle sticks. The toilet paper and paper towel tubes are very light so don't worry about making your frame too sturdy (just no wobbling).

Straight runs

5 I like to use the larger paper towel tubes for the straight parts of my slide. You could build a really long slide instead of a spiraling one!

Curves

6 The curves can be a little tricky, but feel free to trim your tubes a little to make them fit. Don't be afraid of using extra glue or tape!

Reverse drop

7 There are all kinds of fun things you can do with your slide, like the reverse drop I put on the top. To make this just cut a hole in the top of one of your tubes and have a T.P. tube feed into the hole. This takes a little trimming but its a very cool addition to the slide.

The drop

8 The last piece you'll need is "the drop". This is the entrance for your marble, and you can use anything to build it. A paper cup or a shortened T.P. tube would work great. Make sure your drop piece is angled down sharply so that your marble can gain speed and momentum.

Finish

9 The final touches are all that's left! We decided to make some signs out of cardboard and some tools from two toothpicks and some paper. Now you have an awesome Mine Shaft Marble Slide! You can choose any theme for your slide. How about a roller coaster, a jungle, or a cool water park? Use your imagination and have fun!

Boris the Cookie Container Bull

Find these or similar supplies

- 2 toilet paper tubes
- Plastic cookie container
- Empty cardboard cereal box
- Masking tape for customizing
- Coloring supplies or paint

Getting started

1 You can find these cube-like containers at bulk food warehouses or grocery stores... they usually hold lots of cookies or candy. If you can't find one, look around for a similar square or rectangular plastic container. I began by covering mine with a layer of masking tape, my favorite stuff! I also covered Boris' nose.

You don't have to use tape. How about using paint or even some colored tissue paper.

Feet

2 I cut my TP tubes in half, and positioned them at the base of Boris for his feet and taped them on. You could make legs any length you want. I liked the short look!

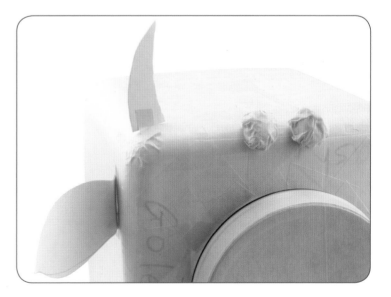

Eyes, ears and horns

3 Boris needed some eyes, ears and horns. I drew these on a piece of cardboard in a shape that I liked, and cut them out. You can make yours as big and goofy as you want. Next simply tape on the horns Bnd ears. Boris is starting to look good! I wadded up some tape into little balls and made Boris some eyes and stuck them on.

Decorate

4 Now it's time to customize Boris. I colored him with a black marker, but you can use paint or anything you can find. I made his ears a bright pink, and added two oval pieces of tape for Boris' nostrils. I colored his eyeballs black and stuck them on top of two circles of white tape.

Spots

5 For Boris' patches, I added white pieces of tape I cut out, but you can just draw them on or attach pieces of white paper you cut out.

Grass

6 Boris looked hungry so I rolled up some green tape into little grass pieces, but you can use paper and color it green if you'd like. Or you can use real grass!

Final touches

7 VOILÀ! Boris the Bull! You can do all sorts of things to customize Boris, so look around for fun things to add, like a tail!

The Milk Carton Sailboat

Find these or similar supplies

- Blue masking tape (optional for customizing)
- Regular masking tape
- String or thread
- Straws or sticks
- Milk carton
- Plastic bag

Getting started

1 Place the carton with the open side facing up. Using a ruler, measure and mark halfway points at each corner. Next, use the ruler to draw a straight line from point to point all the way around the carton. By cutting on this line, you will create a perfectly even boat hull. Now cut your milk carton in half.

Tape your hull

2 Start the first row of tape at the bottom. Tape your carton all the way around, leaving about an inch of excess on the front. Add two or three first row layers, until you no longer see through to any printing on the carton.

A little blue

3 Finish up by adding blue tape for the top row, folding it carefully over and into the inside.

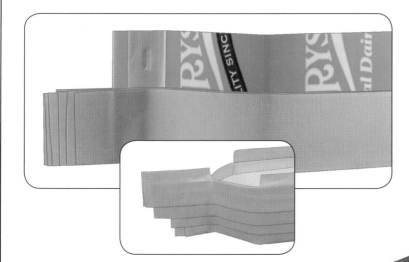

Make your mast

4 I like to use straws for my masts. However, you can use just about anything, like a stick, or a pen or pencil. Start out by covering two straws with tape. This makes them look like real wooden masts. You can add a strip of blue tape at the top for a cool finishing touch.

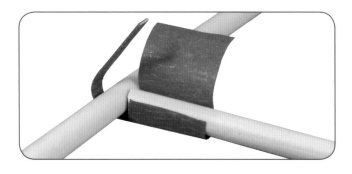
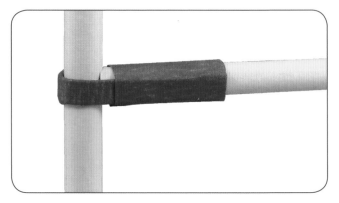

Make your Boom

5 You can make a boom that moves by using a strap that wraps around the mast. Start by cutting a 5–6 inch piece from the second taped straw. To make the strap, try using a 3 inch piece of tape, roll it onto itself lengthwise, and flatten it. Next carefully wrap the strap around your mast and tape it to the boom.

Bowsprit

6 You can attach a bowsprit to the front of your sailboat hull. Use the excess piece of taped straw left over from your boom. Tape it on the front of your ship. Add a layer of blue tape to the front, so that it matches your mast and boom.

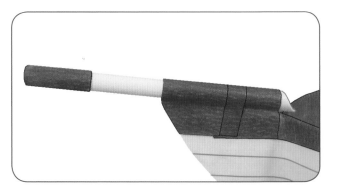

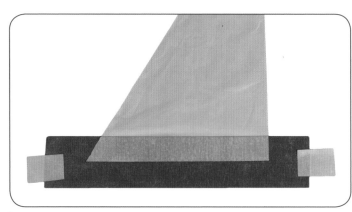

Make the sails

7 Cut your sails from a plastic bag. Hold them in place against your mast to see if they will fit, and make corrections as needed. Do this until you have the shapes and sizes that you like for your sails. Place a piece of tape, sticky side up on a flat surface. It may help to hold it in place by taping the ends down. Now carefully place your sail down the middle of your flipped tape. Punch some holes along the edge for rigging.

Mast slots

8 Another great tip that will make rigging your boat easier is to carefully cut small slots at the top of your mast and on the ends of the boom and bowsprit.

Rigging holes

9 The more time you spend on adding string for your rigging, the more realistic your sailboat will look. I like to start off by making holes at the corners and a few more on each side of the sailboats hull. Use a hole punch, and add holes around the edges of your hull. Try to space the holes as evenly as possible.

Rig your boat

10 Start out by tying a long piece of string to one of the corner holes you punched earlier. Next, run it up and over the mast, laying through your mast slots. Then pull it down and tie it to the opposite corner. Continue this going from corner to corner, side to side and front to back. The most important thing is to use your imagination and be creative!

Newton's World

Finishing Touches

11 VOILÀ! A milk carton sailboat, made from trash! You can add flags and all kinds of cool stuff. It's your project, so be creative and always use your imagination! The most important thing is to have fun!

Cotton Ball Sheep

Find these or similar supplies

- Some old cardboard or paper
- Newspaper
- Masking tape
- Straws
- Cotton balls
- School glue

Getting started

1 This is a very simple project suitable for all ages. You'll want to start out by balling up your piece of newspaper. Crumple it tight, then add a quick layer of tape to hold the shape. You should end up with a mostly round ball.

Build the body

2 The next step is making the legs. First you'll need to poke four holes into your paper ball. I used a pen for this. Then stick in your straws and trim them down to the size you like. Remember to try and make the legs the same length (this will make the sheep sturdier).

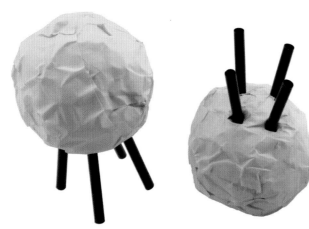

Glue the cotton

3 Now you can start gluing on your cotton balls. Start gluing them using normal school glue. I found that packing the cotton balls tight together gives the sheep a nice fluffy look.

Make the face

4 The final step is making the face. You will only need a few pieces for this. Cut out an oval for the head, some small leaf shaped ears, and two circles for the eyes. Glue or tape these pieces together to make a sheep face. The size and position of the eyes and ears will really change your sheep's expression!

Add your head

5 Now just tape the head right onto the body. VOILÀ! Your sheep is complete!

Big and small

6 This project can also be made using a plastic container as the body. Also any tennis ball or similarly shaped object will work. I made a bigger sheep as an example.

Make a flock

7 Every sheep needs a flock. Remember to have fun!

The Dixie Chickens

Find these or similar supplies

- Plastic or paper cups (big or small)
- Masking tape
- Straws
- Cardboard or construction paper
- Markers or pens for customizing

Getting started

1 To get started making your chicken you will need to draw and cut out its feet, beak, wings, tail and comb (that's the red thing on top of a chickens head). I used an old cereal box for this. You can make your chickens look any way you want, maybe with huge feet or tiny wings. Have fun!

Legs and Feet

2 The next step is to make your chicken's legs and feet. Attach the feet to the straw legs. I punched a hole in my feet first to make the feet more stable. Now take a piece of cardboard and fold it over both straws to secure them in place. Play around with how you want the legs to look. Do you want long or short legs? Splayed feet or pigeon toes?

Wings, beak, tail and comb

3 Now you can tape on your wings, beak, tail and comb. I had lots of fun putting the beak high and low and seeing how the wings looked open or closed. You can add tons of character with your choice of placement.

Goofy eyes

4 The final step is the eyes! These are the most important part of the chicken! You can do all kinds of fun things with the eyes. I have tried big eyes, little eyes, googly eyes, and crazy eyes. Just cut out the shapes you want and go wild! From here you could paint or color your chicken any way you want and be finished.

Tape it up

5 Now for the fancy version! We started out covering everything in a base layer of masking tape. This adds lots of texture to the project and covers the labels from the cups.

Dress it up

6 Next we layered lots of torn pieces of tape on the body of our chickens to give them a feathered look. We then covered all the body parts in tape, making them easier to color on later.

Funny feet

7 We also covered the straw legs in tape to make them look more realistic.

Finish up

8 The final step is the most fun... decorating! We colored all of our chickens with permanent markers, then put on our goofy eyes last. You can make your chicken any color you want, so get creative and customize it! VOILÀ! The Dixie Chicken!

Strike a Pose

The Conga Line

Carton Covered Wagon

Find these or similar supplies

- 1/2 gallon juice or milk container
- Cereal box or some cardboard
- 4 feet thin wire (coat hanger)
- Regular masking tape
- Brown paper bag
- 4 plastic container lids
- 1 big straw
- 4 small straws

Getting started

1 Start out by cutting your juice or milk container in half. This is fairly difficult to do so take your time. I usually use a ruler to mark my cut line all the way around before I make any of my cuts. Then I like to use a utility knife or scissors to make all the cuts. You may have noticed that I used the half with the cap on it. This way when someone sees my covered wagon that will know what it was built from.

Wagon body

2 Next cover your wagon body with tape. I usually spend quite a bit of time taping my projects so that they look cool. Starting from the bottom up, run your tape all the way around. You'll give your wagon a nice wooden look this way.

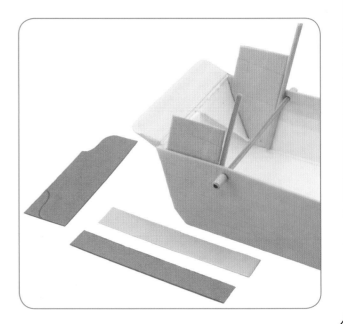

Riding bench

3 I got a little carried away making my bench. The simple way to make it is to cut two pieces of cardboard out for the bench sides and glue or tape them in place. Cut one or two rectangle pieces as shown, cover them with tape and attach the to your bench sides. You can always just fold a piece of cardboard in half for your bench.

Simple cover

4 Making the cover for your wagon is pretty simple. You could just take a piece of paper and cut it to the width that you want, bend it down the way you like, and attach it to the sides of your wagon.

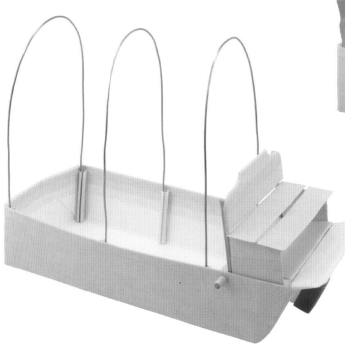

Covered wagon cover

5 I cut six small pieces of straw and glued them into the inside of my wagon, but you can tape them into place if you like. You will need to cut three equal pieces of wire about 14 inches long. Carefully bend them and place them into the straws. Put a piece of brown paper over the top of the frame.

Wheel axles

6 Tape a large straw to the bottom of your wagon, then slide a smaller straw through it. The smaller straw will now turn freely.

Wheels

7 I glued on four lids for my wheels. You can also use cardboard circles as wheels, its up to you.

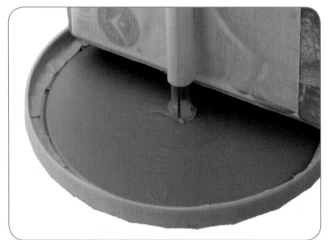

Finish up

8 VOILÀ! A covered wagon! Have fun and remember to try new ways of putting everything together.

Terrance The Turtle

Find these or similar supplies

- Big plastic bowl
- Masking tape
- Some old cardboard or construction paper
- Markers or pens for customizing
- Five toilet paper tubes

Getting started

1 To make this turtle you'll want to find yourself a big plastic bowl. Turn it upside down and tape in the T.P. tubes so that they stick up like legs.

Make a neck

2 When your T.P. legs are done, tape the last tube sticking out like a neck. You may need to cut a little piece of the bowl out to get the neck to fit properly.

39

Decorate it

3 Now you can start to decorate. I covered all my pieces with masking tape (like always) so that I could color the plastic with my colored markers. You can paint your turtle, or maybe cover it with paper, really anything you can think of to dress it up. Have fun!

Make a head

4 To make my turtles head I decided to ball up some tape and stick it to the end of my neck T.P. tube. The nice thing about masking tape is you can mold it like clay to get the shape you want. I used some scissors to cut out a mouth. You could use a small paper cup for the head instead of tape.

Color it

5 The last step for me was the coloring. I decided to stick with the natural green for my big turtle... VOILÀ! A cool plastic bowl turtle. Don't forget to add some cute turtle toes!

The S.S. Milktastic

Find these or similar supplies

- 1 paper towel tube, 2 toilet paper tubes
- Tape (colored tape for decorations)
- 2 smaller boxes (soap box, etc.)
- 2 milk cartons
- String (for rigging)

Getting started

1 Begin by laying out your materials to get the basic shape. This is where you can try different boxes and supplies to see what looks the best. I ended up liking the way two milk containers looked back to back. Then I tried two soap boxes for the cabins and changed one out for a slightly bigger box up front. Next I placed some paper towel and toilet paper tubes on top. These will be smoke stacks. Customize your own ship however you want, the sky is the limit!

Tape it all

2 At this point your ship is ready for assembly, and you can tape all your pieces together and call it a day if you want. I decided to take all my parts and carefully cover them with tape. Most of it took at least two or three layers to completely cover the print on the containers. Try using different colors of tape to dress it up.

Cover the hull

3 You can use layers of tape to make your ships hull look like its made of wood. Just start from the bottom and work your way up.

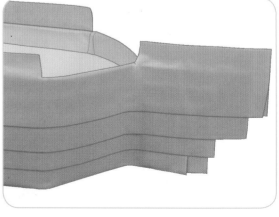

The bow

4 After I covered the main body hull I trimmed the excess tape off of the front and back. Because I left the tape running long I was able to cut the front at an angle that I thought looked cool. You can keep your bow straight or angle it.

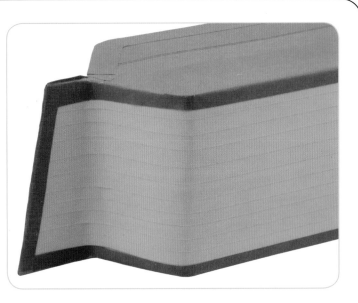

Doors and windows

5 For the doors and windows I tried a few things like drawing them directly on the ship. I ended up cutting them out of some thick paper and colored each one, and then glued them onto my ship, the S.S. Milktastic. Yes... this took me forever.

Windows

6 After I glued all of my doors and windows on, I noticed that they needed to look more like glass, so I carefully colored each window with a light blue marker.

Finished

9 VOILÀ! A very cool ship built from trash! Try using cotton balls for the smoke!

Soap Bottle Fish

Find these or similar supplies

- 1 plastic container
- Old box or some cardboard
- Tape for customizing

Getting started

1 I started out by covering my plastic container with tape. This is a good idea if you plan on dressing your fish up later.

Fins, Flippers and Tail

2 Next I cut out my fins, flippers and tail from an old box. You should play around with different designs, cutting them out and holding them up to your fish body. When you like a look, go ahead and tape it in place.

Rib your fins

3 I spent a lot of time on my fins, flippers and tail before I attached them to my fish's body. After settling on a design I carefully twisted pieces of tape into rope strands. I then taped each strand into place, creating a ribbed looking design. You could always just color your fins to get this effect.

Fish scales

4 I covered my entire fish body with a lots of pieces of masking tape that I had carefully ripped by hand. I tore them into small scales, overlapping each one on top of the other. This created an incredible scaly look. Be warned, it took forever!

Make a mouth

5 For the mouth I wadded up tape, shaping it into the basic mouth that I liked. Then I carefully taped it in place. This took a few layers to get the lips looking fairly smooth and realistic. You can draw on your mouth if you'd like.

Eyes

6 I taped on two water bottle caps for eyes. Later when I had finished coloring the body I cut two cardboard circles out to give my fish some pupils.

Dress it up

7 Now it gets really fun. You can color your fish any way you like! Try new things and see what you can come up with!

Egg Carton Butterfly

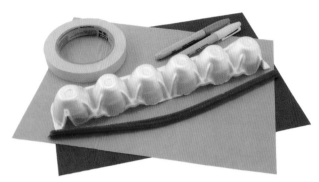

Find these or similar supplies

- Egg carton
- Masking tape or glue
- Colored paper
- Markers or pens for customizing
- Pipe cleaners

Getting started

1 To start this project you'll need to cut out a piece of egg carton. This will be the body of your butterfly, so make it about three "bumps" long. Try to trim the edges evenly.

Color it

2 Now that you've cut out the body it's time to color it. You can use paint or anything you want for this. Have fun decorating!

Legs

3 Cut out six pieces of pipe cleaner and tape or glue them to the inside of the body. Try to make sure they are the same length.

Eyes and antennae

4 To make the eyes you can cut out two circles of white paper. Glue the eyes to the face, then draw on the pupils. To make the antennae just cut two long pieces of pipe cleaner and poke them through the top of the head.

Wings

5 Now it's time to start on the wings. You will need two colors of paper for these. Start out by drawing a wing design, then trace it onto your other color of paper. Now you should have two wings, one of each color.

Cut a design

6 The next step is cutting out a design for your wings. Draw a design that you like, then cut it out of the top wing. I like to start on one side, then fold over my wings so that I can cut out the other side exactly the same.

Glue it

7 Now that you have cut out your design from the top wing, it's time to glue it onto the bottom wing. Make sure they are right on top of each other so that you make one beautiful set of wings!

Attach the wings

8 The final step is attaching your wings to the bug's body. Use a little glue or tape to secure the wings to the middle section of the body. VOILÀ! Your Butterfly is ready to hit the skies!

The TP Flyer

Find these or similar supplies

- Blue masking tape (optional for customizing)
- Cereal box or some cardboard
- Straw or an old pen/pencil
- Clear plastic container
- Regular masking tape
- Toilet paper tube
- 2 paper clips
- 2 pen caps

Getting started

1 Start out by cutting your TP roll at an angle. Your windshield will go here. You could also leave it just the way it is and have a snub nose jet.

Make your windshield

2 I made my windshield from an old plastic container. Find a rounded piece of plastic and trim it to fit on your toilet paper roll. You could also use a plastic spoon for this.

Add the tail

3 Next tape your Flyer's tail on. Cut out a piece of straw and attach it to the back of your toilet paper roll with some tape.

Cut the wings

4 To make the main wing and tail you can use all sorts of supplies. I like to use old cereal boxes. Draw out some wing designs and cut them out.

Landing gear

5 The landing gear is as simple as bending your paper clips into the shape you like and taping them onto the bottom of your Flyer.

Tape it up

6 Put everything together and make sure you like how it looks. Now is the time to make any changes (trimming wings, bending landing gear, etc.).

Decorate

7 This is my favorite step of any project. Have fun customizing your plane. You can use different colored tape like I did or color/paint it.

Finishing steps

8 Now that you are finished decorating it's time to put everything together. Tape or glue all the pieces together and add anything extra you can think of. I added some old pen caps on the wings, so now my Flyer has some jet engines. What can you think of?

Pedro The Pot-Bellied Pig

Find these or similar supplies

- Empty juice or water bottle
- 4 toilet paper tubes
- Regular masking tape
- A pipe cleaner
- Markers or paint

Getting started

1 First you will need to make Pedro's legs. I used some empty toilet paper tubes, and I cut the end of each of them at an angle using some scissors. This way I will be able to attach them to Pedro's body easily.

You don't have to use empty toilet paper tubes. Pedro's legs can be made out of almost anything you can find, like straws, pencils, or even rolled up pieces of paper.

Legs, ears, and tail

2 Next I taped the legs to Pedro's body. You can see how the legs will fit by placing them next to the body, and you can trim the edges of the toilet paper tubes to make them fit just right.

I also completely covered him with a layer of my favorite stuff: masking tape.

Pedro needed some ears, so I cut out two from a piece of paper and attached them to his head. You can also use cardboard or pieces of tape.

Finally, I used a simple pipe-cleaner as a tail, and wrapped it around my finger to make it curly. You can also twist up a piece of paper or tape too.

Color it

3 What color should Pedro be? I thought pink might be a good color for Pedro's body, so I tested a pink marker on him, and he seemed happy. You can use other colors too...the sky's the limit!

I colored Pedro completely with my pink marker. I colored his ears with a darker pink and his pipe cleaner tail too... You can actually color a pipe cleaner with a marker!

Facial features

4 For Pedro's mouth, I rolled up a piece of tape into a thin strip, and shaped his mouth, colored it, and stuck it on. I used some rolled-up balls of tape for Pedro's eyes and colored them black. Finally I drew some nostrils on my piggie! Oink oink!

Pill Bottle Pig

5 Pedro's the proud parent of Percy the Pill-Bottle Piggie-Bank Piglet. He is easy to make too. You can use an empty pill bottle for Percy. You'll need some straws for his legs, a little bit of tape for his ears, and a pipe cleaner for his tail.

You can cut a slot in the top and use Percy as a Piggy Bank. When Percy is full you can unscrew Percy's nose and take out your hard-earned pennies!

Perfection

6 Perfect! It's Pedro the Pot-Bellied Pig! Pedro doesn't take long to make and you can use your imagination for each of his body parts! Have fun!

The Salvaged Sub

Find these or similar supplies

- Some old cardboard or construction paper
- 2 toilet paper and paper towel tubes
- Markers or pens for customizing
- Milk or juice carton
- Small paper cups
- Masking tape
- Egg carton
- Straws

Getting started

1 This project has a lot of creative breathing room. There is really no wrong way to make a Salvage Sub, so play around with your design before you start gluing or taping everything up.

Lay it out

2 This is the basic design for my Salvaged Sub. The toilet paper and paper towel tubes go along the milk carton body, with the small paper cups inserted in the ends. For the front of the tubes I trimmed down some egg carton pieces and stuck them on for a streamlined look. Add a cup and a piece of plastic to the top and you've got a Submarine!

Tape it up

3 Now for my finished Sub I took all my pieces apart and covered everything in masking tape. I used an orange tape for the tubes and the milk carton, and regular tape for all the other pieces.

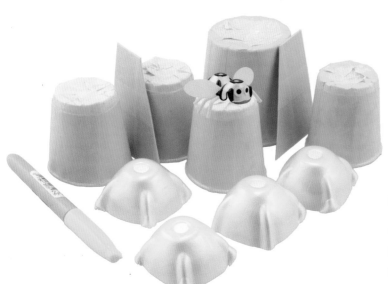

Color it

4 I then colored all of the other pieces (cups, front caps, wings, etc) with a yellow marker. You can always just color your Sub without the tape, or decorate it with paint.

Put it together

5 When I was finished coloring all the pieces I started attaching the parts. The big paper towel tubes go along the bottom, the smaller toilet paper tubes on the top, with some little cardboard fins. The paper cup goes on top, providing the crew with an access hatch.

Dress it up

6 Now at this point I started adding lots of little details to make my sub look cool. The grasper arms are simple to make, just tape two bending straws together and attach them to the sides of your sub. The "hands" on the grasping arms are cut from some tape.

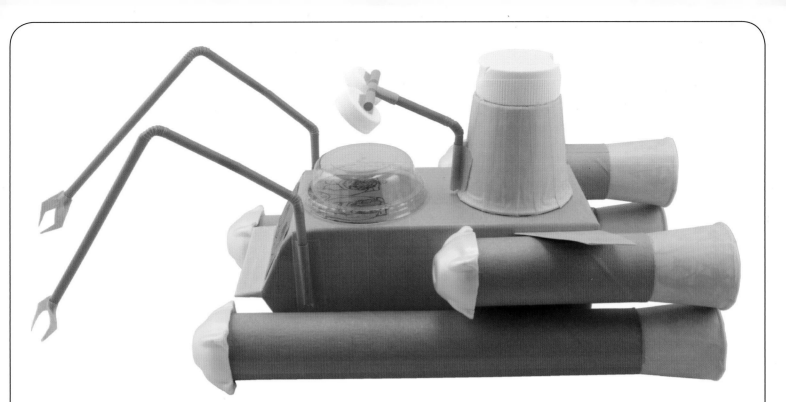

Bubble

7 A plastic lid can become an observation bubble! I also used some straws and bottle caps as my Sub's floodlights. These help illuminate the murky ocean deep!

Front window

8 The last little detail was my front window. You can draw your crew's faces so they can pilot your Salvage Sub through the ocean! VOILÀ! A Salvage Sub!

Milk Carton Mars Rover

Find these or similar supplies

- 1/2 gallon juice or milk container
- Cereal box or some cardboard
- Foil tape
- 2 straws
- 4 container lids
- Stuff for customizing

Getting started

1 Start out by taping your juice or milk container up completely. I used foil tape for my Mars Rover body. You could use regular masking tape instead and color it with marker and make your own designs.

Make your axles

2 Next make four holes on each side of your container that are just a little bigger than the straw thickness. Insert your straws all the way through so that they stick out both sides. These will be your wheel axles. If they do not turn easily, then pull the straws out and make the holes bigger.

60

Wheels

3 You can make wheels out of a piece of cardboard. Simply draw four circles and cut them out. You can do this by taking any circular object and tracing around the edges on your cardboard before cutting them out.

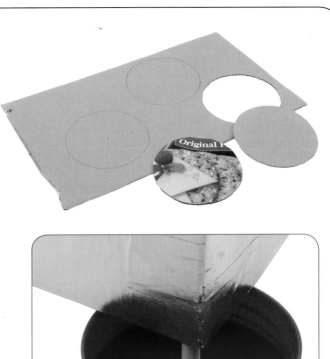

I used four coffee container lids that I had saved for my wheels. If you'd like to use container lids for your wheels, just save four of the same kind, then you can build your own crazy wheeled vehicle.

Attach your wheels

4 I attached my wheels using a hot glue gun. Glue guns are great for crafts like this. If you don't have access to a glue gun then you can carefully tape your wheels onto the axle with small pieces of tape instead.

Finish your wheels

5 Now repeat step four on the other wheels. Make sure to try your best to keep each wheel centered on its axle.

Finishing touch

6 VOILÀ! A four wheeled Mars Rover! You can start rolling it around or dress it up. This is my favorite part of any project. I looked through my recycling bin and found a detergent push button top. I attached it to the top of my Rover and now it's a futuristic piece of equipment! For my windows I cut out small pieces of cardboard from a popcicle box, then covered them with some black tape and attached them. Have fun and see what you can come up with.

LooLe-Maxx Video Camera

Find these or similar supplies

- 2 cardboard or cereal boxes
- Empty water bottle or paper cup
- Masking tape (for customizing)
- 4 paper plates

Getting started

1 I love to film people making fun crafts, and my favorite tool is the excellent high quality LooLe-Maxx HD Imagitron camera! My version of the camera is very flashy and has lots of extra features, but this project is very simple to make. You can use almost anything you can find to build it.

This is the type of craft that is great for all ages. Younger kids may just be able to tape the pieces together, while older kids can make more complicated versions and spend more time dressing it up. Always use your imagination and experiment with using different supplies and different ways of putting it together.

Just tape your paper cup to the front of one box and another box to the back. If you'd like to use an empty water bottle for your camera lens, cut it in half with scissors and tape the bottom half of the bottle to the front of the main box.

Tape it up

2 Next tape up your LooLe-Maxx with masking tape. I used blue but you can use any color. I drew markings around my lens like a real camera. You can leave the base of your water bottle lens clear or color it black.

Buttons and knobs

3 I need a fine level of control when I am filming crafts, so my LooLe-Maxx needs lots of buttons and dials. I used bottle caps for knobs and strips of cardboard covered with tape for sliders.

Film

4 I keep my high-quality LooLe-Maxx film in the film cannisters on the top of my camera. To make these I cut the ridges off of four paper plates so that they would match when I put them together. I covered them with tape, taped a pair of plates together, and did the same for the other pair.

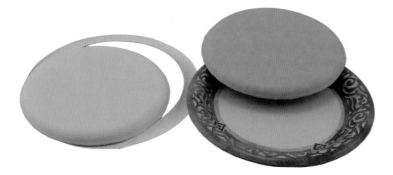

Cannister Box

5 I added another box to the top of my LooLe-Maxx, taped it up and cut a slot in the top for my film cannisters. Then I slid my cannisters into the slot. You can tape them in place if you'd like.

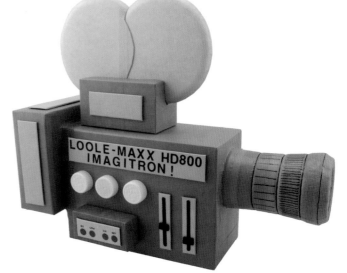

Detail it

6 I added all sorts of controls and knobs and dials all over my LooLe-Maxx to give me lots of fun options when filming. You can add anything you like!

Finished

7 VOILÀ! My LooLe-Maxx HD800 Imagitron camera!

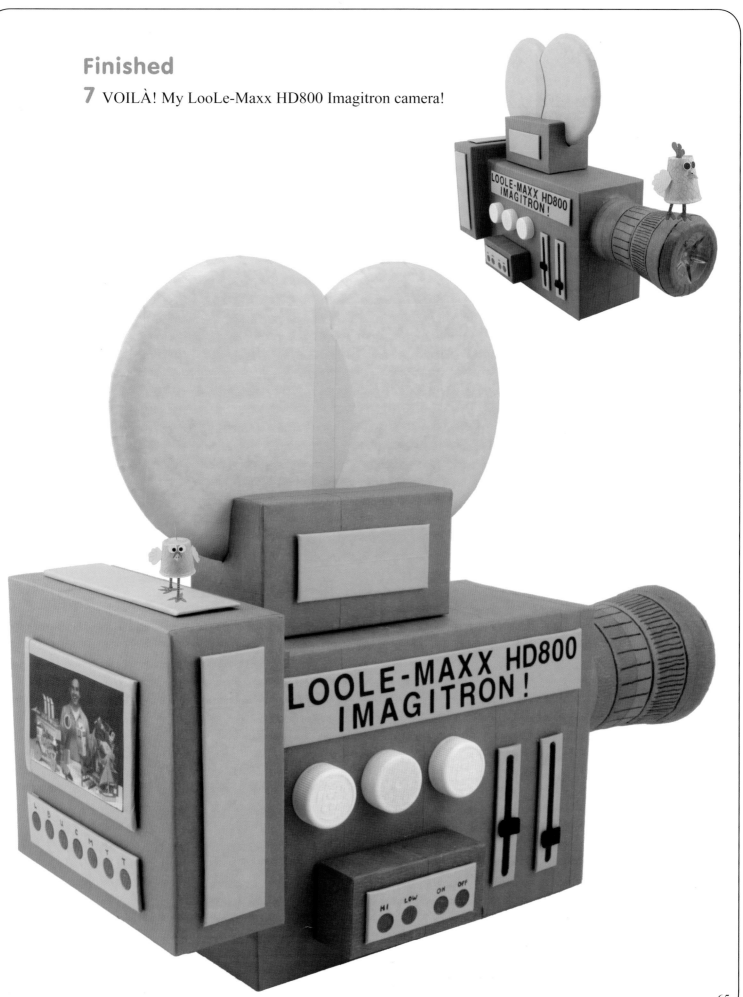

Camping Compass

Find these or similar supplies

- Magnet (look on the refrigerator)
- Needle or a piece of paper clip
- Leaf or something small that floats
- Paper plate or something to hold water

Getting started

1 Start out by magnetizing your needle. Any object (like a needle or a paperclip) that sticks to your magnet can be magnetized. With your needle laying down on the table, hold one end down firmly. Then place your magnet onto the needle. Remember, the needle wants to jump to the magnet.

Magnetize

2 Always slide the magnet in ONE direction along your needle. While holding your needle down, start sliding the magnet away from the finger that you are using to hold it down. Make sure to apply some pressure to the magnet as you slide it along the needle.

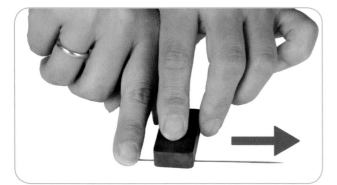

3 Keep sliding

4 All the way past the end

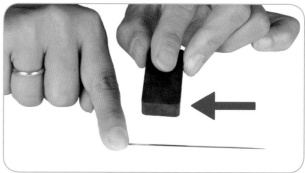

5 Now lift your magnet up and away from the needle. Bring it around and start all over again. All you are really doing is rubbing the needle in one direction.

6 Repeat step 2 through 5 about 50 times. Yes... that's a lot, but it will insure your needle is properly magnetized. Now see if your needle is magnetized by touching it to another piece of metal, like another paperclip. If it sticks, then you are ready to make a compass. If not, magnetize it again, but rub even more times.

Put it together

7 Now its time to make your compass. I found a leaf to use as my compass's floating base. You could experiment with other small floating objects to see how they work and use whichever one works best. Place your leaf onto some water so that it floats and is in the center. Then very gently place your magnetized needle onto the leaf. Try to keep your needle, leaf, and paper plate very still. If you've magnetized your needle enough, it should begin to spin and point towards the NORTH.

Finished

8 VOILÀ! A camping compass. There are all kinds of ways to make compasses, so try experimenting with different supplies and ways of putting it together. Have fun!

Simple Turtles

Find these or similar supplies

- Some old cardboard or construction paper
- Markers or pens for customizing
- A bowl (paper or plastic)
- Masking tape

Getting started

1 This project has a very basic design. Take a paper bowl (or plate) and use it as your turtle's shell. Cut out some feet, a tail, and the head from some cardboard or paper.

Tape them on

2 Next tape your pieces to the bowl. To get your turtle to stand upright you can have your legs angled down along the sides of the bowl.

Decorate

3 Now its time to color your turtle. You can decorate however you'd like, I chose to color my turtle with markers but you can paint or glue on anything.

Eyes

4 I cut out some paper circles and glued them to my turtles face. Its easy to make some fun cartoon eyes this way.

Make more!

5 Your turtle is complete. These turtles are really quick to make... so I made two!

Egg Carton Ornaments

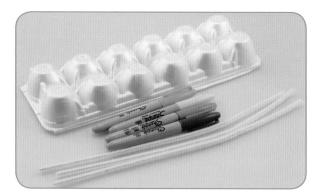

Find these or similar supplies

- Egg carton
- Pipe cleaners (or string, wire, or paper clips)
- Pens for customizing

Getting started

1 This is a great way to reuse egg containers. These ornaments are very fun and simple, so the whole family can do them.

Start out by cutting your egg carton into individual pieces. If you don't have an egg carton you could use small paper cups for this project.

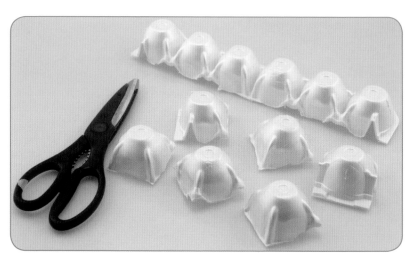

Make your hangers

2 Pipe cleaners make great ornament hooks. If you can't find these around your classroom or house, you can also use some paper clips, a small piece of wire, or even string.

Bend the end of your pipe cleaners to make hooks for your ornaments. The pipe cleaners poke right through the top of the Styrofoam.

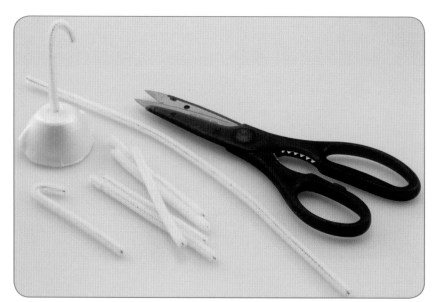

Paper cups

3 Another great way to make ornaments is to use small paper cups. You can assemble them the same way. Poke a small hole on the top and insert your hanger. Then dress it up!

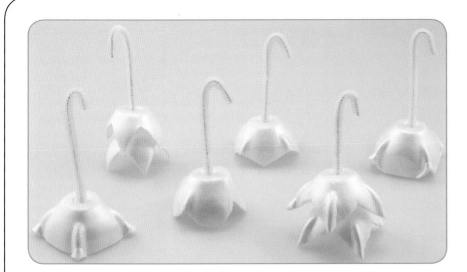

Cut into shapes

4 Next you can trim your ornaments into fun shapes. I played around with circles, triangles, even stacking two together. The sky is the limit, so have fun and see what you can come up with.

Decorate

5 VOILÀ! Egg Carton Ornaments! The final step is the most fun. Decorate your ornaments using paint or markers for a fun and festive look. Have fun trying new color combinations and designs!

A Duck-bill Platypus

Find these or similar supplies

- Water bottle
- 4 plastic forks
- Old box or some cardboard
- Tape for customizing

Getting started

1 Start out by giving your water bottle a base layer of tape. I wrapped it a few times so you could not see through the tape.

Cut out the bill

2 Next cut out your duck-bill's mouth. This took me a few tries before I got the look I liked. Now tape them onto and around the mouth of your bottle. I added a few more layers of tape to get my bill to blend in with the body.

Tail

3 Like the duck-bill's mouth, the tail took some adjusting. You can hold up the tail and trim it to your liking.

Feet

3 For my duck-bill's feet I used forks. All you need to do is cut most of the handle off of each fork and tape them in place. You could use almost anything for the feet. How about plastic spoons?

Dress it up

4 After installing all the pieces on your duck-bill platypus you can dress it up. There is no limit to what you can do, so be creative and try different supplies. I added a few more layers of tape, carefully blending the different pieces together.

Eyebrows and eyes

5 To make the eyebrows I twisted some pieces of tape up, trimmed them, shaped them and placed them on both sides of my duck-bill's head. Then I carefully covered them with torn pieces of tape. The eyes are easy, just cut out two small paper circles and stick them under your eyebrows.

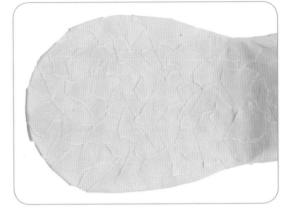

Cover with tape

6 Next I covered the bill with tape, making sure to have as few seams and overlaps as possible. I ended up tearing lots of little pieces of tape to cover my platypus body. This gives the project some texture and looks really cool.

Decorate

7 I used permanent markers to color my platypus. They're great for coloring masking tape. Use whatever you like and always remember to have fun!

Viking Long Boat

Find these or similar supplies

- 1 quart or bigger carton
- 1 straw & 12 skewers
- Regular masking tape
- String or thread
- Paper bag

Getting started

1 Start out by cutting your milk carton in half. Try to keep the sides as even as possible.

Dragon head

2 Draw out a cool design for the front of your ship. This can be a dragon head like mine, or anything you want. Once you have a design you like, cut it out and tape it to the front of the hull.

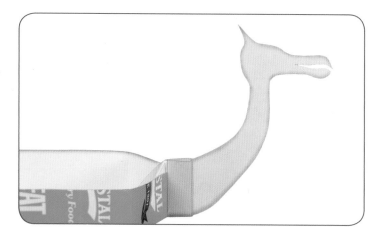

Tape your hull

3 I like to layer masking tape along the side of my ship to make it look like wooden planks. To do this you just start at the bottom and do one layer, then work your way up. This is a great way to cover up the packaging so that you can color your ship with ease later on.

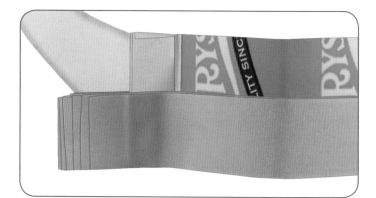

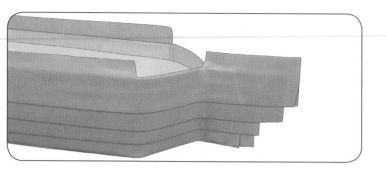

Build A Rudder

4 Simply draw out a tail rudder you like, then cut it out and tape it onto the end of your Viking ship. You can make a rudder that actually moves by taping up some toothpicks and putting them in a straw, as shown below.

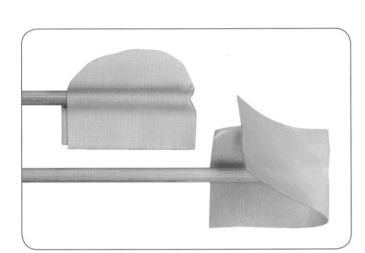

Paddles

5 You can use toothpicks or wooden skewers for your paddles. I just trim my handle down to the size I like, then I double over a piece of tape at the end to make my paddle. Trim the tape into a shape you like.

A Sail

6 Cut out a square piece of brown paper (grocery bags from the store work great). Line the edges with tape, then punch holes around the sail so you can rig it up later.

Mast

7 I like to use straws for my mast, but you can use just about anything. Start out by covering the straw with tape. This will make it look like real a wooden masts. I find it helps to cut out some slots in the top of my mast to tie my string to.

Rigging

8 I like to punch some holes in the corners of my boats then run string from side to side. You can do your ships rigging any way you want, there is no wrong way. Take your time and have fun!

Finish

9 You can add and color shields and all kinds of cool stuff. It's your project, so be creative and always use your imagination. The most important thing is to have fun!

Fresh Water Bottle Fish

Find these or similar supplies

- Regular masking tape
- Blue masking tape
  (optional for customizing)
- Colored or plain paper
- Colored markers
- 2 Straws for optional stand

Getting started

1 Start out by taping your water bottle up completely. I used the blue masking tape for the main body color. You could use regular masking tape instead and color your fish with a marker and make your own designs.

Make fins and flippers

2 To make my tail, fin and flippers, I found a piece of colored craft paper. As always, you can use whatever you find. I drew my fins and then cut them out. Try making different designs! Cut them out and hold them up to your fish to see which ones you like the best.

Install your fins

3 Now start putting it together. Attach your tail, fin and flippers using small pieces of tape. Try moving them around until you have a look you like.

Eyes

4 Eyes are great because everyone makes them differently. I tried using bottle caps and tacks, but I settled on making my own. I used wadded-up pieces of masking tape that I shaped by hand, and then carefully covered with tape. I then colored them and taped them into place. See what you can come up with!

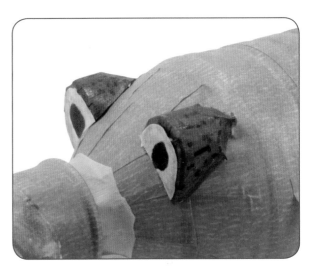

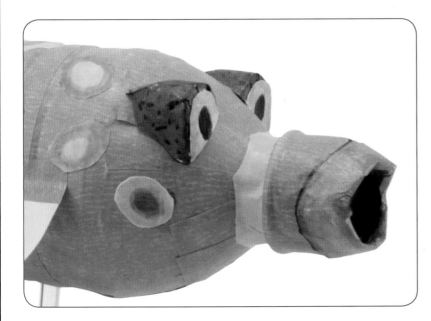

Mouth

5 To make the mouth I carefully wrapped a piece of tape around the bottle cap and folded it in on itself, shaping as I went. After several layers and some trimming I colored it.

Spots

6 I cut out spots for my fish from regular masking tape. I made them different shapes and sizes. I stuck them on and tried to space them evenly. You could try making stripes or something else instead.

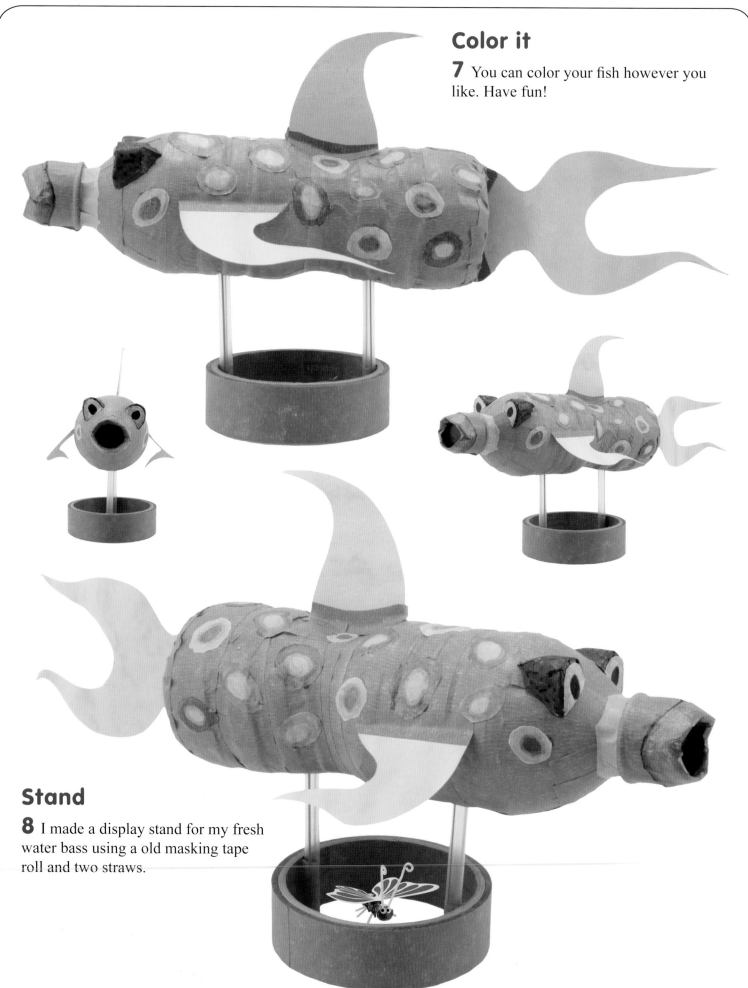

Color it

7 You can color your fish however you like. Have fun!

Stand

8 I made a display stand for my fresh water bass using a old masking tape roll and two straws.

The Trash Bot

Find these or similar supplies

• Anything you want! You can use old boxes, cans, plastic containers, toilet-paper or paper-towel tubes, milk cartons, egg cartons, bottle caps, string, or packaging material. The most important thing you'll need is your imagination!

• Tape or glue

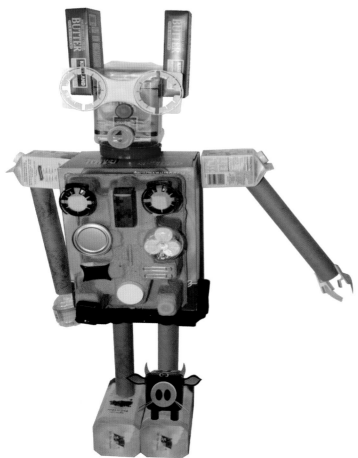

Getting started

1 The Trash Bot is one of those projects where you can really use your imagination when putting it together. You can use almost any discarded or recyclable material to make his body parts. He doesn't even need to have two arms or legs... maybe your Trash Bot will have wheels!

This is a great project for a classroom or family to build together. Each person can find a single part for the Trash Bot, and customize it the way they would like before they attach everything together.

Lay it out

2 For my Trash Bot, I used a larger empty cereal box for his torso, and empty paper-towel tubes for his arms and legs.

I used some unusual packaging material for his chest and the top of his legs. I found some milk cartons for his shoulders and a cookie container for his head.

Next I found lots of bottle caps and plastic pieces around the house for various robot buttons.

I laid all these out before I put my Trash Bot together.

Put it together

3 Before I put my Trash Bot together, I covered his head, torso, and feet with aluminum foil. You can use tape, or you don't have to cover yours at all. I covered his other body parts with colored masking tape to make him look nice.

Then I put him together using a combination of tape and glue. You don't have to use glue, but if you have some handy it's useful for reinforcing his body parts.

Finish up

4 VOILÀ! My Trash Bot! He's never really finished, so I can always come back and add new parts if he needs them. As always, look around for different supplies... it's your project, so make him however you want! Remember, the sky's the limit, and always have fun!

Randoph The Reindeer

Find these or similar supplies

- 1 empty plastic bottle
- Straws for legs
- Cereal box or some cardboard
- Regular masking tape
- Cotton ball (for the tail)
- Markers, pens, or paint for customizing

Getting started

1 Everyone knows Rudolph the Red-Nosed Reindeer, but not many people are as familiar with his rambunctious remote relative, Randolph, complete with a rosy red bottle nose. The first thing I did was make Randolph's legs by taping some straws together. I used three straws for each leg, but you can use less if you'd like. I also cut my straws down to a smaller size.

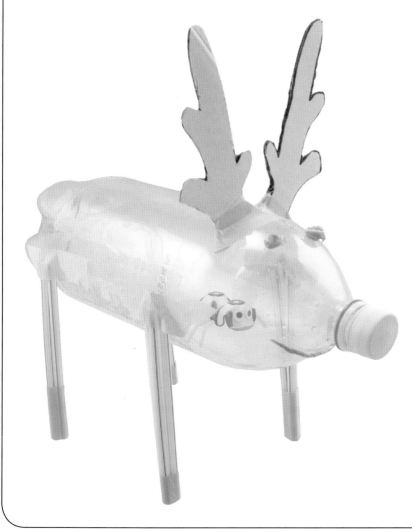

Make the basics

2 Randolph's body is simply an empty 2-liter soda bottle, but you can use a smaller water bottle and make a mini version instead. I taped Randolph's legs to the side of his body like you see here.

I cut out some pieces of cardboard in the shape of his antlers, and positioned them on Randolph's head. I also wadded up a few pieces of tape for his eyes.

Next I rolled up a long piece of masking tape into a long thin strip for his mouth. You can make his mouth any shape you want.

At this point you can be finished or you can start decorating.

Cover with tape

3 I like to cover my crazy creatures with masking tape because it makes it easier to decorate them. I covered Randolph's body with a layer of regular masking tape, including his nose. I actually covered his nose with multiple layers of tape to give it a thick, bulbous look.

You can cover his legs with a thick layer of tape as well to make sure that Randolph won't have any problems standing up.

If you don't have enough tape, you can just start customizing Randolph now and use paint to cover him.

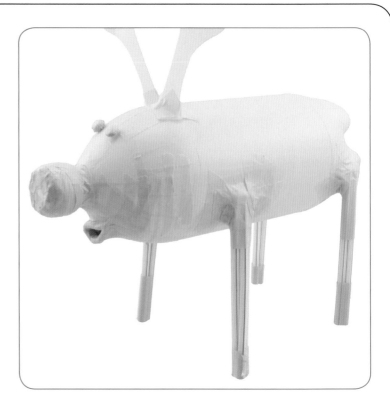

Customize it

4 Customizing Randolph is a lot of fun. I spent a lot of time on his fur by cutting out strips of masking tape into small triangles and layering them over his body. I used a marker to color his body and to give him a furry look.

You can just color his body with markers or paint if you'd like.

I also cut out some small pieces of cardboard and made some ears for Randolph and taped them on.

Color it

5 I colored his rosy red nose with a red marker. I also colored his mouth red, and his hooves black. I made Randolph's eyes black, but you can use any color.

I colored his antlers and ears with a brown marker.

Finally you can add a cotton ball tail by wadding up a piece of tape and attaching the tail to his body with it.

Finished

6 VOILÁ! Randolph, the rambunctious remote relative of Rudolph the Red-Nosed Reindeer!

The PT Racer

Find these or similar supplies

- 1 paper towel tube
- Old box or some cardboard (for wheels)
- 2 straws
- Tape (colored tape for decorations)

Getting started

1 Start out by making your PT Racer wheels. Take an old box or piece of cardboard and draw four circles (two big ones for the rear wheels and two small ones for the front). Then carefully cut out all four wheels. Find the center of each wheel and make a small hole for your straw axle to slide through. Try not to make the hole too big or the wheels might wobble.

Axles

2 Next I made four holes on my PT tube using a hole punch. Try to make all of your holes as level as possible. Now insert your axle straws. I had to adjust my holes a little so that the straws turned freely.

Wheels

3 Now slide your wheels onto your straws. Trim the straws down, making sure to leave some excess so you can adjust the wheels and tape them on later.

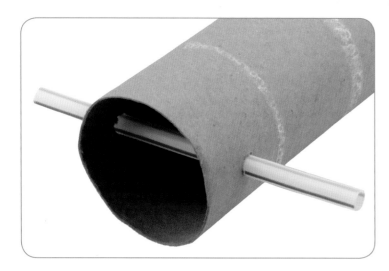

Front

4 I decided to make the front of my PT Racer look speedy by building a front end. I made a paper cone, trimmed it, and stuck it in the front. You can make your front end look any way you want! Its your project, so experiment and have fun!

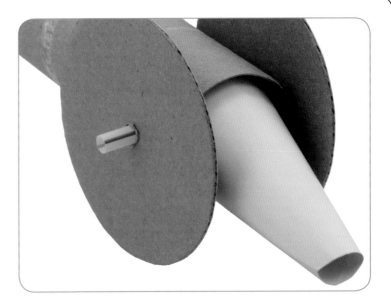

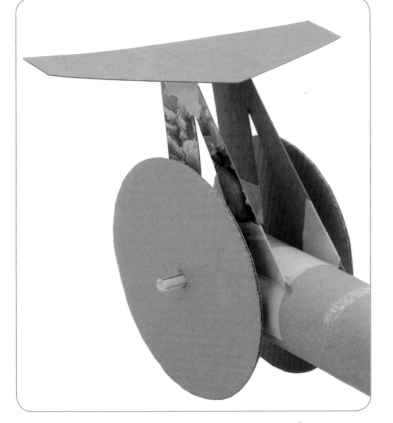

Tail

5 How about a tail? I cut out some different designs, held them up, and decided on this look. This is where you can get really creative. VOILÀ! Your PT Racer is ready to roar past at daring speeds!

Dress it up

6 Now for my favorite part of every project... dressing it up! For my PT Racer I used three colors of masking tape. I disassembled all the pieces and carefully covered everything with varying colors of tape. You can experiment with markers or stickers or anything you can imagine! The sky is the limit!

Racing stripes

7 My PT Racer was looking pretty plain, so I cut strips of different colored tape for a racing stripe look. You could try polka dots, flames, or lightning bolts for a fun decorative twist.

Margaret the Spray Bottle Turkey

Find these or similar supplies

- 1 empty spray bottle
  (make sure you wash it thoroughly!)
- Cereal box or some cardboard
- Regular masking tape
- Markers or paint

Getting started

1 First make sure that you wash your spray bottle completely before you use it. All you really need for Margaret is a spray bottle and something for her tail. Her tail can be as simple as attaching a paper plate, or you can cut out some tail feathers from paper or cardboard. Attach your feathers, add some eyes, color Margaret, and you are done!

Make your feathers

2 For Margaret's tail feathers, I played around with different supplies and shapes until I found what I wanted. I ended up making her tail feathers out of pieces of a cereal box that I cut out. But you can use a paper plate or anything else you can come up with.

Cover with tape

3 Next I covered each of Margaret's feathers and her body with a layer of masking tape. You don't have to use tape; you can just color her tail and body later with markers or paint.

Gobble gobble beak

4 Margaret needs a beak, so I took some masking tape and attached it to the spray bottle nozzle. I wadded it up and shaped it to give her a nice beak. I added some masking tape to her head to giver her a wrinkly turkey look. For Margaret's body, I ripped off small pieces of tape and layered them all across her surface to give her feathers.

Gobble gobble feet

5 Margaret needs turkey feet, so I cut out a pair from some cardboard. I attached a small piece of straw to the top of the feet, cut holes in her base, and pushed them in. But you can simply tape or glue Margaret's feet in place.

Finish up

6 I colored Margaret's tail with some stripes and added some details to make them look more like real turkey feathers.

When I was done coloring Margaret, I attached her tail pieces by gluing them all together first, one at a time (in a fan shape) and then attached the top-most piece to her body with glue.

Wattle

7 Gobble Gobble! Wait, Margaret needs a chin... a turkey's chin is called a "wattle", and I thought the best wattle for Margaret would be a red balloon. Voila! It's Margaret the Gobble Gobble Red Wattle Spray Bottle Turkey!

Mini Biplane

Find these or similar supplies

- 1 toilet paper tube
- Cereal box or some cardboard
- Regular masking tape
- 1 small paper cup

Getting started

1 Start out going to the back of this book and draw or trace the template for the mini biplane. You can also just draw your own designs for the wings and tail onto a piece of old cardboard. It's your plane, so be creative. You could make your wings larger or make the shape different... perhaps dragon or bird wings will do!

Make the parts

2 Trace or draw out the pieces onto some cardboard and cut everything out.

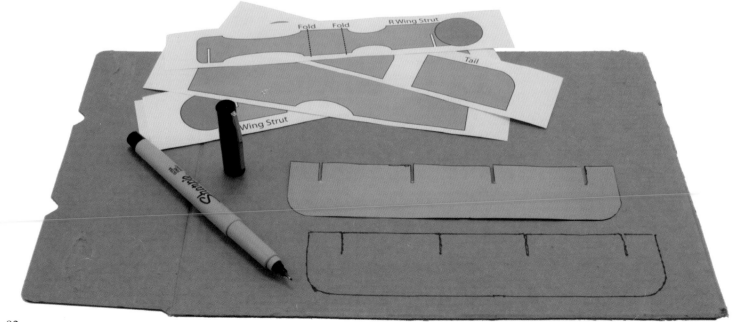

Tail Section

3 Tape the tail section to your rear wing. I like to cut three slots at the end of my TP tube for the tail section to slide into. You could tape your tail section directly onto the TP tube if you like. I also cut out a little cockpit area in the middle section for my pilot to sit in and fly the biplane.

Wing struts

4 Now take your wing struts and bend them into place, and then slide them onto the lower wing, fitting them into slots you cut out. I put the bigger end of the struts closer to my main body — and now I magically have landing gear. Finally, tape the lower wing and struts to your main body.

Top wing

5 Next, you need to take your top wing and tape it onto the wing struts. Make any necessary adjustments, and then tape it all together. Your mini biplane is almost complete!

Propeller

6 Now it's time to build the propeller! Take your small paper cup and cut it in half. Glue or tape your propeller piece onto the bottom of your cup. I trimmed my cup to fit right onto the front of my TP tube.

Dress it up

7 Finish up your plane by taping on your propeller to the front of your TP tube. At this point you can decorate your mini biplane. Maybe your mini biplane needs some racing stripes or some thunderbolts... the sky is the limit! VOILÁ! A cool mini biplane to fly around the house!

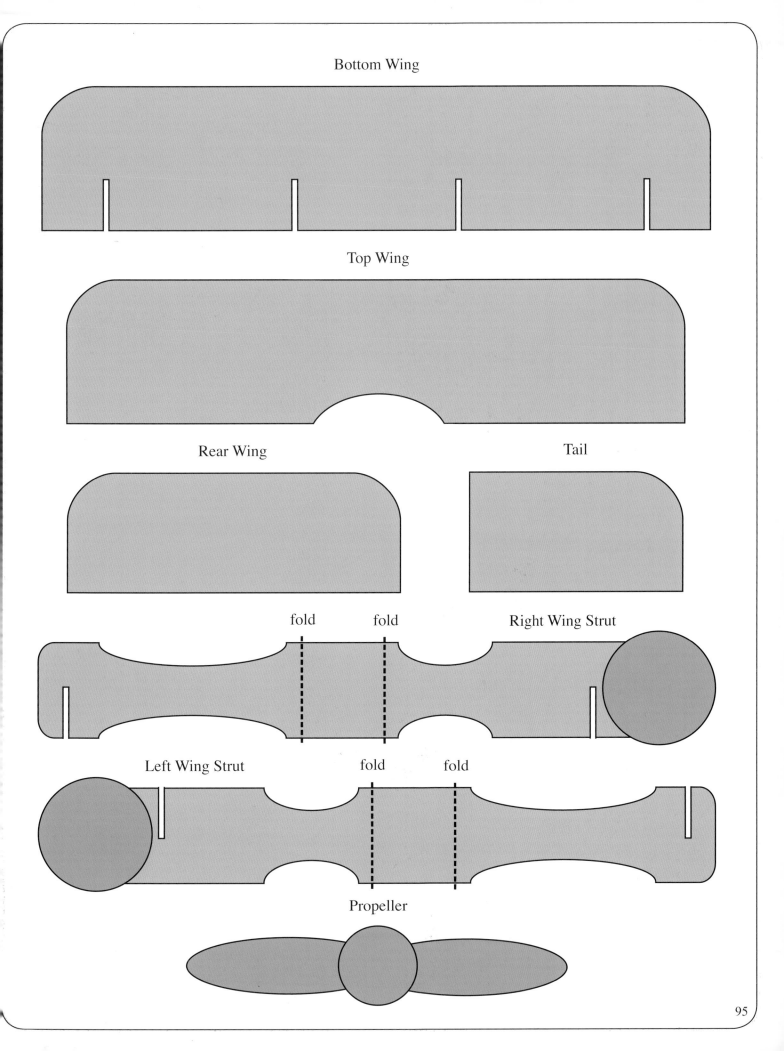

Bottom Wing

Top Wing

Rear Wing

Tail

fold   fold

Right Wing Strut

Left Wing Strut   fold   fold

Propeller